CREATIVE WRITING

PRACTICE WORKBOOK
WITH ASSESSMENT TESTS

Ages 6–7

7+

CREATIVE WRITING

FOR INDEPENDENT SCHOOL ENTRANCE

PRACTICE WORKBOOK WITH ASSESSMENT TESTS

7+

FAISAL NASIM

Contents

About This Book — 3

Section 1: What to Expect
Starting Point – Writing Task — 4
Types of Writing:
    Story — 5
    Continue the Story — 5
    A Story Based on a Picture — 7
    Diary Entry — 8
    Report — 10
Marks Breakdown — 12

Section 2: Skills Practice
Understanding the Task — 13
Planning — 14
Paragraphs — 16
Past and Present Tense — 17
First and Third Person — 18
Conjunctions — 20
Pronouns — 21
Sentence Openers — 22
Capital Letters and Full Stops — 23
Commas — 24
Speech Marks — 25
Adjectives — 26
Verbs — 28
Adverbs — 30
Similes — 32
Alliteration — 34
Weather — 36
Emotions and Feelings — 37
Characters — 38
Settings — 39
Spelling — 40
Handwriting — 42
Checking Your Work — 43

Section 3: Test Practice
Tasks 1–4 — 44
Tasks 5–10 — 45

Section 4: Answers and Guidance
Answers — 46
Glossary — 51

About This Book

7+ Entrance Exams

7+ entrance exams are used by a number of independent schools to assess pupils for admission in Year 3. Pupils usually sit the exam midway through Year 2. Since there is no standardised process, the format, timing, content and structure of the exams vary widely from school to school. However, the exams tend to be based on the same syllabus and, in a vast majority of cases, they include some form of writing assessment.

Creative Writing in 7+ Exams

The English section of a 7+ entrance exam usually consists of a comprehension task and a writing task. This book is designed to help your child prepare for the writing task.

Writing tasks allow for the measurement of how a child thinks as well as their potential for empathy and logical thought. As such, this section of an exam can be challenging.

The tasks often have a tight timeframe (e.g. 15–30 minutes), so your child should concentrate on quality over quantity and try to showcase what they have learnt in a focused way. They should be encouraged to stick to the question and ensure they are addressing it directly. Regurgitating a previous piece of creative writing, or descriptive section, just because it got praise at school or good marks in a mock exam, should be discouraged. Examiners will notice a 'prepared piece' instantly and could knock off marks if it bears no relation to the question.

Make sure you visit the relevant school's website. Most schools publish information about their selection procedures and exams on their sites and some even include example exam papers.

About This Book

This book is designed to help pupils prepare for the writing part of a 7+ exam. Many children at this young age find it difficult to know where to start when faced with a blank page and some instructions. This book aims to break down the writing task into its component parts, making it more comprehensible and approachable for young children and giving them a clear framework within which they can confidently express their ideas.

The book takes a step-by-step approach, clearly explaining the various elements that your child needs to be aware of and providing plenty of opportunities for practice.

Your child should complete the practice exercises and tasks in this book independently. However, help with reading the instructions where necessary and ensure they understand what to do. They should write their answers in a separate notebook or on sheets of lined paper. The answers to all practice exercises and tasks are given at the back of the book.

Starting Point – Writing Task

Here's a short writing task. It will give you an idea of what you can already do and which areas might need a little more practice.

Writing Task – 25 Minutes

Write a story with the title 'The Amazing Teapot'. You can use the image alongside to help you.

 Helpful Tip...
Think about these questions before you start writing:
- Why is the teapot amazing?
- Who are the main characters in your story?
- How will you make your story interesting and exciting to read?

Go through your story with an adult and give yourself a mark out of 5 for each of the items in the checklist below.

Don't worry if you found some parts of this task difficult. You will be working through each of the items in the next section of this book, so you will have plenty of opportunity to practise and develop your skills!

	Score	See pages:
I followed the instructions and wrote a relevant story.		5–15
I completed my story within the given time.		14
My story has a beginning, middle and end.		14
I divided my story into paragraphs that begin in the correct place.		16
I used correct punctuation, including capital letters, full stops, commas and question marks.		23–25
I included interesting and exciting adjectives and adverbs.		26–31
I included a simile and some alliteration.		32–35
I spelt my words correctly and used good handwriting.		40

Types of Writing

In your 7+ exam, you may be asked to write a story, a diary entry or a report. Here's a little more information about each of these types of writing, including example questions and answers.

Story

A story is a piece of fiction. It is not real – it is imagined. It can contain different characters and settings. Often, an interesting story will be about a problem that needs solving or a quest that needs completing!

Helpful Tip...
- Before you begin writing, spend some time planning your story (see page 14).
- Good stories usually have a clear focus. Think of one or two key ideas that you will include in your story. By staying focused, your story will be easy to read and understand and you won't run out of time. It will also help you to write in detail about the main ideas and create rich descriptions.
- You should try to make your story exciting for the reader. You can do this by using creative vocabulary and including interesting settings and characters.

Continue the Story

Your writing task may ask you to continue a story. You may be asked to continue the story used in the comprehension section of the exam or you may be given a few sentences to begin your story.

Example

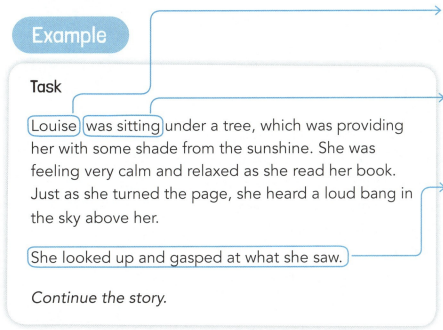

Task

⟨Louise⟩ ⟨was sitting⟩ under a tree, which was providing her with some shade from the sunshine. She was feeling very calm and relaxed as she read her book. Just as she turned the page, she heard a loud bang in the sky above her.

⟨She looked up and gasped at what she saw.⟩

Continue the story.

→ You can see that the story is written in the third person (see pages 18–19), so you must make sure you continue to write in the third person.

→ You can see that the story is written in the past tense (see page 17), so you must make sure you continue the story in the past tense.

→ The text ends on a point of suspense. You must continue the story directly from this point and describe what Louise saw and what happens next. By doing this, you will show the examiner that you have understood the text and are able to write a logical and interesting story.

Example Answer

A bright blue kite came hurtling down from the sky towards her. Louise thought it was going to hit her on the head so she swiftly ducked out of the way. Luckily it missed and instead landed on its tip in the ground just in front of her. Its long tail was wrapped around the branch of the tree above, like a coiled snake. → Past tense / Written in the third person / Adverb / Simile

"I wonder who it could belong to," Louise wondered angrily. → Description of feelings

"It's ours!" came a voice from behind the tree. "We thought we had lost our beautiful kite, but you have found it for us," said a small, delicate girl, with long black hair and sea-green eyes. She was followed by an older boy who had the same coal-coloured hair and green eyes. They looked like brother and sister. → Character description

Louise, who had been worried that it was going to hit her on the head, was annoyed at their carelessness. She thought they should be more responsible and scowled at them. → Use of pronoun / Interesting verb

"We're sorry," the boy said. "We weren't trying to hit you."

He explained that a gigantic gust of wind had blown the kite out of his hand. He could not hold on to the string because the wind was too blustery, powerful and strong. He had not expected it on such a sunny day. → Description of weather / List of three adjectives (punctuated correctly)

Once Louise realised that it had just been an accident, she smiled at them both and helped them to unwrap the kite's tail from the tree. Apart from a very small tear in the top corner, it was undamaged and still able to fly. So they all ran far away from the tree and climbed to the top of a nearby hill, where they could catch the breeze and fly the kite without being a danger to anyone.

7+ CREATIVE WRITING

A Story Based on a Picture

Sometimes you may be asked to write a story based on a picture or a series of pictures.

Example

Task

Write a story that begins based on the events shown in this storyboard.

Helpful Tip...
- The pictures show an alien spaceship hovering over a school playground. The story should begin by describing these events and then move on to what happens next.
- The story could be past or present tense (see page 17) and it could be first or third person (see pages 18–19) as these details are not given.
- Specific details in the images can be included in the story. For example, in this case, it could include a description of how the spaceship looks based on how it is shown in the images.

Diary Entry

A diary entry is a record of the things you did over the course of a day.

Diary entries allow you to describe what you did on a certain day. They are also a great opportunity to write about your thoughts and feelings.

Helpful Tip...
- Diary entries are usually written in the past tense (see page 17) because you are writing about things that have already happened.
- Diary entries are usually written in the first person (see pages 18–19) because you are writing about things that happened to you.
- A good diary entry will not only include details about what you did but also about your opinions and feelings.
- Just like stories, you can make your diary entries interesting for the reader by using creative vocabulary and vivid descriptions.
- You might sometimes be asked to write a diary entry from the viewpoint of an imaginary character.
- Diary entries sometimes begin with the phrase, *'Dear Diary'*.

Example

Task
Imagine you are a doctor. Write a diary entry about a day at work that you remember.

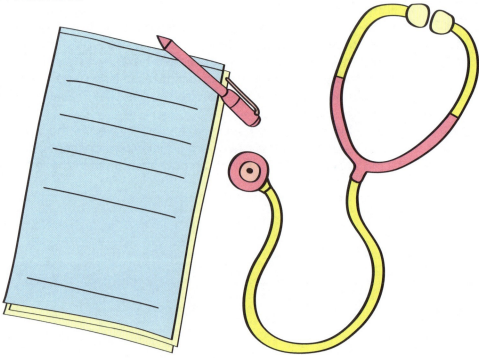

Example Answer

Dear Diary,

I've had such a busy day at the hospital today. I didn't even have time for my lunch! As soon as I arrived, there was an emergency. An ambulance came roaring into the car park, its lights flashing like blue sequins and its siren sounding like a screeching bird. There was a frail old lady in the back. She had fallen over in the shopping centre and broken her ankle. She was in a lot of pain. I gave her some painkillers, put her leg in plaster and helped her into a wheelchair. She let me sign her cast with my favourite purple pen. I scrawled 'Dr Jo' in big, bold letters along her leg.

Then, I had to visit my patients in the hospital ward to make sure they were okay and getting better. One man had his family visiting him and he introduced me to them. They wanted to bring his dog in to see him, but I explained that pets were not allowed inside the hospital. Instead I said he could go into the hospital courtyard and see his dog there. This caused him to smile. It made my day to be able to make him happy.

Next, I taught a first aid class to a group of pupils from the local school. They were all very interested to learn how to clean and dress a wound and how to tie a sling. One boy said he was scared of blood and he nearly fainted when I used some red paint to create a pretend cut on someone's arm. I don't think he will be a doctor when he grows up!

I now feel exhausted and am ready for bed. I hope tomorrow won't be so busy… and that I will have time for my lunch!

Annotations:
- Written in the first person and informal (use of contraction)
- Past tense
- Sentence opener
- Simile
- Simile
- Alliteration
- Interesting verb
- Pronoun
- Sentence opener
- Description of feelings

Report

A report is a non-fiction text. This means that it is factual – it is not made up.

Helpful Tip…
- A report should contain lots of factual information.
- Think about how you will plan your report (see page 14) so that the information is clearly organised.
- Reports are often written in the present tense (see page 17) as they are describing facts.
- Whilst reports are non-fiction, you can still make them interesting and exciting by including lots of creative description and vocabulary.
- If you have a choice of topic, make sure you choose one that you know a lot about so you won't find it hard to think about facts and information to include.

Example

Task

Write a report for your school magazine with the title 'My favourite animal'.

Example Answer

My favourite animal is my pet dog Trixie, a Tibetan Terrier. She has dark, curly hair, which gets all over the place. When she sits on my lap, she looks like a plate of black spaghetti. She needs grooming every day, which can take quite a long time, so my sister and I take it in turns to brush her.

Tibetan Terriers are warm, cute and loyal pets, and they are great around children. That is why my parents chose Trixie, so she would get on with us. They love to play and are very springy. I really enjoy taking her for walks, although her coat picks up lots of leaves, twigs and mud, which means we have to wash her in the bath when we get back. This can be annoying sometimes, when all I want to do is have a bath myself. We always have to wash her first and then my mum uses the hairdryer to dry her. She has so much messy hair, it would take ages to dry on its own.

My mum told me that Tibetan Terriers were originally bred to herd flocks of sheep and to guard monks who live in the high mountains of the Himalayas. I can't imagine Trixie coming from such a faraway place, but she does make an excellent guard dog. If a stranger comes to the house, she will always bark to warn us. She is never aggressive and I know she would never bite anyone. She just makes a lot of noise.

This is why Trixie is my favourite animal. I couldn't imagine living without her as she is part of our family and we all love her very much.

Marks Breakdown

The writing task in the 7+ exam will be marked by an examiner. They will give you a mark based on how well you performed in several areas. For example, if there are 25 marks available in total, they might be awarded as follows:

Following the instructions correctly	10 marks
Punctuation and spelling	5 marks
Vocabulary	5 marks
Presentation and handwriting	5 marks

These are the areas you need to focus on when completing the writing task to make sure you score as many marks as possible!

Following the Instructions Correctly

There are a lot of marks awarded for this. It's very important that you read the task instructions carefully and make sure you follow them. For example, if you are asked to write a story about an alien but you write a report about cats, you will lose a lot of marks! It's important that you don't write memorised sentences and paragraphs – you must write a direct response to the given instructions.

Punctuation and Spelling

Marks are awarded for using accurate punctuation and spelling. For example, you must use capital letters, full stops, commas, question marks and speech marks in the correct way. You must also take care to spell words correctly.

Vocabulary

Marks are awarded for using interesting and exciting words. You can do this by including plenty of descriptive adjectives and adverbs. You may also wish to include a simile or two and some alliteration.

Presentation and Handwriting

Marks are awarded for making your writing clear and easy to read. You can do this by dividing your writing into paragraphs and by making sure your handwriting is neat.

Understanding the Task

Before beginning your writing task, it's important that you read the instructions carefully and understand what you need to do.

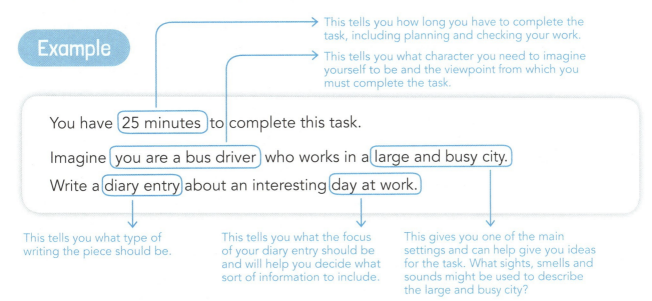

As you can see, you can learn lots of useful information just by reading the task instructions carefully.

Practice

Read the task below and then answer the questions.

> You have 30 minutes to complete this task.
> Write a report about your favourite television show.
> Make sure you clearly describe the show and explain why you like it.

Q1. How long do you have to complete the task?

Q2. Is your task to write a diary entry, story or report?

Q3. What should your writing be about?

Q4. What other pieces of useful information do the instructions contain?

Planning

Once you have read the task instructions carefully, it's time to make a plan so you can organise your ideas and use your time efficiently.

Your piece of writing should have three main parts: a beginning, middle and end. Therefore, your plan should also be divided into these three parts. This structure can be used for all the types of writing covered in this book.

Helpful Tip...

You may not have a lot of time to write a detailed plan but it's always worth jotting down a few ideas. You don't need to write full sentences in your plan – you can just write brief notes.

Generally speaking, if your writing task is 25 minutes or less, you should spend about 2 minutes on your plan. If your task is longer than 25 minutes, you may wish to spend up to 5 minutes writing a more detailed plan.

The planning grid below is for an adventure story. It lists the type of information that might be included in each part of the story.

Beginning	Middle	End
• name of main character • where the story takes place (setting) • names of any other characters • some information about the problem to be solved / quest to be completed	• What happens to the characters as they solve the problem / complete their quest – what difficulties do they face and do they overcome them? • Are any new characters introduced?	• What happens to the characters in the end? • How do they feel about their adventure? • How does the story end?

Example Plan

Here is a plan for a story with the title 'The Jungle Adventure'.

Beginning:
- main character – Lily
- setting – a magical jungle
- Lily's friend, Ben, captured by evil monkeys
- Lily must rescue Ben!

Middle:
- Lily sets out into jungle
- uses special traps and tricks to capture monkeys
- monkeys reveal Ben's location
- Lily rescues Ben and escapes evil monkey, King Bonobo

End:
- Lily and Ben return home safely
- happy and relieved, tired and sleepy

What do you think of this plan? Does it sound like it would make an interesting story?

Practice

Write a plan for each task below.
Try to spend no more than 2–3 minutes on each plan.
If it helps, you can draw a planning grid to help you organise your thoughts and ideas.

Q1. Write a story with the title 'The Talking Tree'.

Q2. Write a diary entry describing the best day of your life.

Q3. Write a report about a city you have visited.

Paragraphs

Paragraphs help you to divide and structure your work, making it clearer and easier to understand.

Helpful Tip...
You can use paragraphs to separate the beginning, middle and end of your piece of writing. Therefore, you should have a minimum of three paragraphs.

Show the beginning of a new paragraph by starting a new line and leaving an empty line before it.

Example

Jamie was exhausted after a long day of playing and swimming at the seaside. He brushed his teeth in a daze and had just enough energy left to change into his pyjamas. He then collapsed into bed and fell asleep instantly.

The next morning, Jamie was jolted awake by the piercing squeal of his alarm clock. It was already eight o'clock and he would have to hurry if he was going to be on time for school!

Practice

Q1. Draw lines to divide the following short story into three paragraphs.

Jimy woke up very early in the morning. He excitedly put on his clothes, ate his breakfast and said goodbye to his mother before leaving the house to catch the bus. When he arrived at the stadium, Jimy found his friends standing outside. They were all as excited as Jimy about the big match. They entered the stadium and took their seats. The match was full of twists and turns and the boys found it very entertaining. Afterwards, Jimy said goodbye to his friends and returned home. That evening, he helped his mother prepare dinner and they watched a show on the television. Jimy was so exhausted that he fell asleep on the sofa!

Past and Present Tense

You will need to decide whether to write in the past or present tense.

Diary entries are usually written in the past tense because you are writing about things that have already happened, e.g.

> This morning, I ate beans on toast for breakfast.

Reports are often written in the present tense because you are writing about your thoughts and about facts, e.g.

> Leopards are my favourite animal. They usually hunt at night.

Stories can be written in the present tense or the past tense. You will sometimes be able to decide which tense to use by reading the task.

Example Tasks

Write a story about a king who lived in England one thousand years ago.

Helpful Tip...
In this case, the story should be written in the past tense because it's about a king who lived a long time ago.

Write a story with the title, 'The Ice Town'.

Helpful Tip...
This story could be written in the present or past tense. However, it's very important that the whole story is written in the **same** tense!

Practice

For each of the following tasks, state whether you should write them in the **past tense** or **present tense.**

Q1. Imagine you are an alien that visits earth. Write a diary entry about the first day of your visit.

Q2. Write a story called 'The Enchanted Forest'.

Q3. Write a report about your favourite hobby.

First and Third Person

Make sure you read the task instructions carefully as they will often make it clear whether you need to write in the first person or third person.

First Person

First person means writing from the main character's viewpoint or writing about you, e.g.

> I went home to clean my boots.

Common first person words include: I, me, my, mine, myself, we, us, ours.

Diary entries are usually written in the first person.

Third Person

Third person means writing as though you are watching the story happen around you, e.g.

> He went home to clean his boots.

Common third person words include: he, she, him, her, his, hers, himself, herself, they, them, theirs.

Stories can be written in both the first person and the third person. Look at the examples on the next page.

Example Tasks

Imagine you are a detective. Write a story about an interesting case you had to solve.

Helpful Tip...
In this case, the story must be written from the viewpoint of the detective, so it must be written in the first person.

Write a story about a boy who gets smaller every day, instead of bigger.

Helpful Tip...
In this case, the story must be about a boy, so it must be written in the third person.

Write a story with the title, 'The Amazing Machine'.

Helpful Tip...
In this case, the story could be written in first person or third person. However, you must stick to your choice – do not switch between the two!

Practice

For each of the following tasks, state whether you should write them in the **first person**, **third person** or **either**.

01. Write a story called 'The Mad Scientist'.
02. John and his father went to the circus. Write a diary entry from John's viewpoint about the day.
03. Write a story called 'My Adventure on the Moon'.

Conjunctions

Here's an example of two simple sentences:

    The boy went to the park. The boy played on the swings.

You can use a conjunction to connect the information in these two sentences and form one, longer sentence:

    The boy went to the park and played on the swings.

There's nothing wrong with using simple sentences. However, by using conjunctions to join them together, you can improve your writing by making it easier and more interesting to read.

Conjunctions can also help to make your writing clearer and easier to understand. For example, here are two simple sentences:

    The girl was happy. The girl received a present.

You can use a conjunction to connect these two sentences:

    The girl was happy because she received a present.

In this case, the conjunction explains why the girl was happy, making the meaning easier to understand.

Some of the most common conjunctions are: and, but, because, so.

Practice

Rewrite each pair of sentences using a conjunction to connect them.

Q1. Tim wanted to play football.
Sara wanted to play rugby.

Q2. The rocket was not built correctly.
It crashed into the sea.

Q3. Malik went to the bathroom.
He wanted to wash his face.

Q4. Ada entered the kitchen.
She opened the fridge.

Q5. The dog barked loudly.
It saw someone outside.

Pronouns

The following sentence uses the word 'James' too many times!

> James opened the box and then James called his friends to come and take a look at what James had found.

It can be made less repetitive by using pronouns:

> James opened the box and then he called his friends to come and take a look at what he had found.

Common pronouns include: I, me, we, us, ours, you, yours, she, he, hers, his, her, him, it, they, them, theirs.

You can only use a pronoun if the noun you wish to replace has already been mentioned. For example, take a look at this sentence:

> I called Sarah and told Sarah the good news.

If you replace both mentions of Sarah with a pronoun, it will no longer be clear who was called:

> I called her and told her the good news.

Instead, you can improve this sentence by replacing the second example of Sarah with a pronoun:

> I called Sarah and told her the good news.

Practice

Rewrite the following sentences replacing nouns with pronouns where necessary.

Q1. Gini went to the hospital because Gini was not feeling well.

Q2. Sam and Tom wolfed down the food because Sam and Tom were hungry.

Q3. The man helped his daughter because his daughter was stuck.

Q4. The builder removed the post so that the post was no longer blocking the path.

Q5. I opened the box of chocolates and ate all of the chocolates.

Sentence Openers

Avoid beginning each sentence in the same way, as this can quickly become boring for the reader. By varying the way you start your sentences, you can make your writing more interesting and memorable.

Read this short passage:

> Ben looked around the room. He could not find what he was looking for. He opened all the drawers and ransacked the cupboard. He peered under the bed and checked the rubbish bin. He found it!

Now read this version:

> Ben looked around the room. Frustratingly, he could not find what he was looking for. First, he opened all the drawers and ransacked the cupboard. Next, he peered under the bed and checked the rubbish bin. Finally, he found it!

Sentence openers can help to show the order of things, e.g. next, then, firstly, secondly and finally.

Sentence openers can be used to link the ideas in two sentences, e.g. therefore, meanwhile, nevertheless and although.

Helpful Tip...
Sentence openers can also be adverbs, which help to add interesting description to your sentence. For example, you could begin with words such as: nervously, happily, slowly, suddenly and carefully.

Practice

Q1. Copy the passage below and add sentence openers to make it more interesting and engaging for the reader.

> Layla heard a knock on the door. She jumped back as she was not expecting anyone. She approached the door. She peered through the glass to see who it was. She gasped when she saw the face.

Capital Letters and Full Stops

Punctuation is the name given to the symbols used to make writing clearer and easier to read and understand. It is very important that you use correct punctuation when completing your writing task.

Capital Letters

Capital letters are used at the beginning of a new sentence, e.g.

There were many people in the room.

Capital letters are also used at the beginning of names of people and places, e.g.

My brother James decided to go to London.

Helpful Tip...
'James' is the name of a person so it begins with a capital 'J'.
'London' is the name of a city so it begins with a capital 'L'.

Full Stops

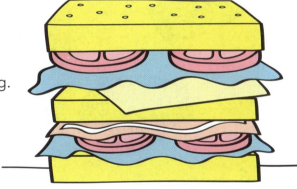

Full stops are used at the end of a sentence, e.g.

Lara ate her sandwich at home.
Gail ate her sandwich at work.

Practice

Rewrite the following sentences adding capital letters and full stops in the correct places.

Q1. he wanted to come yesterday but he forgot

Q2. helen and peter struggled to finish the gigantic chocolate cake

Q3. my best friend went to paris last year

Q4. she did not want to go to the cinema but we did

Q5. ali decided to stay at home oliver decided to go out to play

Commas

A comma is used to separate the items in a list, except for the last two items, which are separated with the word 'and', e.g.

> Muhammad went to the shop and bought oranges, apples and bananas.

> Rupert asked Maria, Ben, Lucy, Amy and David.

Each item in a list may consist of more than one word, e.g.

> Freddy ate a cheese sandwich, a packet of crisps and a chocolate bar.

Helpful Tip...
The three items are:
- a cheese sandwich
- a packet of crisps
- a chocolate bar.

These are called noun phrases.

Practice

Rewrite the following sentences including commas in the correct places.

Q1. The boy put on his gloves hat and scarf because it was cold outside.

Q2. May wanted to go to the park the museum and the shops.

Q3. The hungry monkey ate the bananas the oranges the apples and the pineapples.

Q4. Raji changed her clothes brushed her teeth and ate her breakfast.

Q5. The vicious wolf had large claws thick fur and wicked eyes.

Speech Marks

Speech marks are used to show which words are actually being spoken by a character.

Only the words spoken should have speech marks around them – do not include any words that describe who is saying it or how they are saying it.

Look at these examples:

"I want to brush my hair! said David angrily." ✗

"I want to brush my hair!" said David "angrily". ✗

"I want to brush my hair!" said David angrily. ✓

The third sentence is correct because the speech marks are around only the words that David speaks.

Helpful Tip...
Handwritten speech marks look a little bit like a small 66 and 99.

Practice

Rewrite the sentences below adding speech marks in the correct places.

01. The astronaut said, I saw many amazing things in space.
02. Can we listen to the radio? asked Vin.
03. I simply can't believe it! Soni exclaimed breathlessly.
04. You may leave once you have cleaned your plate, she declared firmly.
05. Rebecca shouted, I'm coming too!

Adjectives

Adjectives are describing words. You can use them to make your writing come alive in the mind of the reader. Compare these two sentences:

    The boy lived in the house at the end of the street.

    The mysterious boy lived in the haunted house at the end of the spooky street.

Which of the above sentences was more interesting and exciting to read? Yes, the second one!

Adjectives are like a superpower that can transform ordinary writing into amazing writing! You can make adjectives even more powerful by combining them, e.g.

    The moon looked gigantic in the sky.

    The moon looked gigantic, shiny and wonderful in the sky.

In the second sentence, three different adjectives are used to describe the moon, making it even more interesting and informative.

When combining adjectives, remember to use ones with **different** meanings so you provide lots of new information for the reader, e.g.

    The moon looked gigantic, shiny and wonderful in the sky.

    The moon looked gigantic, huge and large in the sky.

The adjectives used in the first sentence all tell the reader something different about the moon. The adjectives used in the second sentence all mean the same thing, which is pointless, so it is not as impressive or interesting!

Helpful Tip...
Try to use creative and interesting adjectives in your writing. For example, the adjective 'nice' gets used a lot. However, the following alternatives are more creative and specific:

pleasant   splendid   agreeable   delightful   lovely   enjoyable

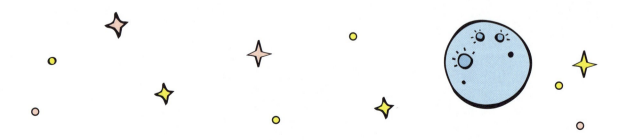

Practice

Q1. Rewrite the following passage adding in adjectives to make it more exciting and interesting.

Helpful Tip...
Remember, you can add more than one adjective to describe something if you wish!

> The dinosaur had claws and teeth. It had muscles and a tail. The dinosaur was a hunter. It used its eyes and nose to hunt for prey. The animals in the jungle all feared the dinosaur and tried to avoid it. Some were luckier than others!

Q2. Sort the following interesting adjectives into four groups by meaning: **good**, **bad**, **big** and **small**.

Helpful Tip...
If you are not sure of the meaning of any of the adjectives, look them up in a dictionary.

immense   wretched   enormous   amazing   tiny   dreadful
miniscule   unpleasant   marvellous   miniature   massive
fantastic   gigantic   colossal   stupendous   terrible
terrific   huge   awful   minute   microscopic   outstanding
disagreeable   diminutive

Q3. For each of the following adjectives, write three more interesting alternatives.

(a) scared
(b) happy
(c) sad
(d) pretty
(e) angry

Verbs

Verbs are 'doing' or 'being' words. A full sentence should contain at least one verb.

Like adjectives, verbs are a great way of making your writing more interesting. Take a look at this sentence:

"I don't want to go!" said Henry.

The verb 'said' could be replaced with another more specific verb to make the sentence more interesting to read, e.g.

"I don't want to go!" bellowed Henry.

"I don't want to go!" cried Henry.

"I don't want to go!" wailed Henry.

"I don't want to go!" screamed Henry.

Helpful Tip...

Try to use creative and interesting verbs in your writing. For example, the verb 'like' gets used a lot. However, the following alternatives are much more creative and specific:

admire   cherish   adore   treasure   appreciate   prize

Practice

Q1. Read the passage below and underline all the verbs.

> Sophie and her friend went on holiday. They spent their days on the beach. They ate ice cream for lunch every day and read lots of interesting books. It was a fantastic holiday!

Q2. Rewrite each of the following sentences twice. Replace the verb with a different, more interesting alternative in each version.

Helpful Tip...
Think about how the different verbs you choose change the meaning of each sentence.

- **(a)** Fred jumped over the wall.
- **(b)** The boy ate a pancake.
- **(c)** Linda sat on the chair.
- **(d)** Tariq threw the rock into the pond.
- **(e)** Rose was talking with Faisal.

Q3. Sort the following interesting verbs into four groups by meaning: **walk**, **run**, **laugh** and **cry**.

Helpful Tip...
If you are not sure of the meaning of any of the verbs, look them up in a dictionary.

weep	giggle	sprint	wail	sob	chortle	bolt	stroll
cackle	bawl	hoot	saunter	race	chuckle	dash	trudge
strut	shuffle	snivel	amble	scurry	dart	snicker	blubber

Q4. For each of the following verbs, write three more interesting alternatives.

- **(a)** look
- **(b)** said
- **(c)** think
- **(d)** go

Adverbs

Adverbs are mainly used to describe verbs.

Adverbs tell you how, where, when or how often something is happening. For example:

- how – quickly, quietly, reluctantly, elegantly, cheerfully
- where – here, there, nearby, everywhere, nowhere
- when – now, first, last, later, today, tomorrow
- how often – occasionally, regularly, weekly, frequently, constantly.

As you have probably noticed, many adverbs end with the letters 'ly'. Here are some more examples:

> The lion approached the vehicle threateningly.
> Victoria passionately defended the environment.
> Paul hesitantly lifted the lid.

Helpful Tip...
Think about how the adverb shown in colour in each sentence above develops the meaning of each sentence and how it provides more information for the reader.

Practice

Q1. Read the passage below and underline all the adverbs.

> Robert swiftly put on his jacket and rushed outside. He could see the light flickering continuously in the distance. He sprinted towards it as quickly as possible.

Q2. Rewrite each of the following sentences twice.
Add a different adverb to each version.

You can choose adverbs from the box below or use one of your own.

> thirstily   beautifully   crazily   loudly   happily   merrily
> tunelessly   foolishly   desperately   gracefully   innocently
> strongly   blindly   lazily   brightly   rapidly

Helpful Tip...
Think about how the different adverbs you choose change the meaning of each sentence.

(a) The two cats drank the milk.
(b) Edward believed in ghosts.
(c) The young man whistled as he walked across the road.
(d) The bird flew from one forest to another.
(e) Sunlight poured through the windows into the room.

Q3. For each example below, write an interesting sentence including the adverb.

Helpful Tip...
If you are not sure of the meaning of any of these adverbs, look them up in the dictionary.

(a) accidentally   (g) obediently
(b) politely   (h) wearily
(c) bravely   (i) wisely
(d) hesitantly   (j) fortunately
(e) doubtfully   (k) angrily
(f) eventually   (l) ruthlessly

Similes

Similes compare one thing to another using the words 'like' or 'as'.

Using similes is a great way to make your writing more expressive! For example:

John ran across the field as fast as a rocket.

The cloud looked like a great ball of cotton wool.

Think about the images that these two sentences create in your mind. Your aim should be to create similarly clear and interesting images in the minds of your readers!

To create a simile, first think of the object or action you wish to describe, e.g. a ball.

Next, since ball is a noun, think of an adjective to describe it, e.g. The hard ball.

Finally, think of another noun that your chosen adjective could describe, e.g. A hard rock.

You can now combine these to form a simile, e.g. The ball was as hard as a rock.

Helpful Tip...
Remember that your simile must include the words 'as' or 'like' to make the comparison.

Practice

01. Add a noun phrase to complete each of the following similes.

- **(a)** as big as…
- **(b)** as cool as…
- **(c)** as small as…
- **(d)** as brave as…
- **(e)** as fresh as…
- **(f)** as heavy as…
- **(g)** as slippery as…
- **(h)** as tall as…
- **(i)** as straight as…
- **(j)** as cold as…
- **(k)** as sweet as…
- **(l)** as hard as…
- **(m)** as red as…
- **(n)** as bright as…
- **(o)** as smooth as…
- **(p)** as delicate as…
- **(q)** as light as…
- **(r)** as strong as…

Q2. Write a simile to describe each of the following pictures.

Q3. For each example below, write a full sentence including the simile.

(a) like an angel
(b) like a dream
(c) like a wild animal
(d) like a fish
(e) like a mountain
(f) like a log
(g) like a rocket
(h) like a pancake
(i) like a wolf
(j) like a volcano
(k) like a slug
(l) like a flash
(m) like the wind
(n) like a glove
(o) like a firework
(p) like glass
(q) like a bull
(r) like a mouse

Alliteration

Alliteration is when a group of two or more words start with the same letter sound. For example:

dirty dogs
prancing ponies
silver stones

Using alliteration is a great way to grab the reader's attention and make your writing more descriptive and memorable!

Here is a short nursery rhyme. Try to read it accurately and quickly:

Three grey geese in a green field grazing,
Grey were the geese and green was the grazing.

This rhyme contains plenty of alliteration of the letter 'g'. This makes it enjoyable to read and more interesting for the reader. You can use the same technique in your writing!

You don't need to use lots of alliteration in your writing task but it can be nice to include a few examples. It's especially useful when creating names for your characters (see page 38).

Helpful Tip...
Remember, it is the starting sound rather than the letter itself that is important. So 'whole head' and 'naughty knight' are examples of alliteration as the words begin with the same sound. In contrast, 'kind knight' is not an example of alliteration as the words do not begin with the same sound.

It's really fun to try to create your own examples of alliteration. Here are a few examples:

Ben's beagle barked.
My muffin is mouldy.
Henry's house is humongous.
Liz let me look at her lion.
The cotton cloud covered the silky sky.
They own an old oven.
India is an incredible country.
William walked to the workshop.

Practice

Q1. Write down two adjectives to describe each of the following words making use of alliteration.

- **(a)** lion
- **(b)** snail
- **(c)** house
- **(d)** aeroplane
- **(e)** rocket
- **(f)** field
- **(g)** window
- **(h)** homework
- **(i)** police officer
- **(j)** doctor
- **(k)** ambulance
- **(l)** corn
- **(m)** fruit
- **(n)** pear
- **(o)** kitchen

Q2. For each example of alliteration below, write an interesting sentence containing the given phrase.

- **(a)** trusty tools
- **(b)** fiendish fox
- **(c)** burning bright
- **(d)** wicked wizard
- **(e)** salty snack
- **(f)** purple petal
- **(g)** fiery flame
- **(h)** wild wilderness
- **(i)** ruby rose
- **(j)** leaping leopard
- **(k)** soft sand
- **(l)** crunchy crisps
- **(m)** colourful kite
- **(n)** soaked street
- **(o)** hovering helicopter
- **(p)** jumping giraffe
- **(q)** drooling dog

Weather

You've learnt lots of different techniques to make your writing more interesting and descriptive. Now you're going to look at how you can apply these techniques and ideas.

When completing your writing task, depending on the story title, you may wish to include a description of the weather. Describing the weather is a great opportunity for you to show off all your new skills!

Read this description of a rainy day:

> The rain streaked silently across the wide windscreen. Great groups of grey clouds gathered on the horizon. Suddenly, a bolt of lightning flashed in the distance and this was followed by rolling thunder that sounded like a growling tiger. I felt impressed, awestruck and a little bit frightened!

Practice

Q1. Read the description of a rainy day again. Underline:
- **(a)** two examples of alliteration
- **(b)** one simile
- **(c)** one adverb that describes when something happened
- **(d)** one conjunction.

Q2. Write a short passage of description based on each picture below. Try to include as many different descriptive techniques as you can. Show off your skills!

(a)

(b)

(c)

(d)

Emotions and Feelings

Another great opportunity to show off your descriptive skills is when writing about emotions.

When completing your writing task, you may wish to describe how your characters are feeling or your own feelings if you are writing in the first person.

Read this short passage describing how Beth felt after playing in a tiring football match:

> Beth was completely exhausted. Her tight muscles ached and throbbed and it felt like a drum was beating in her head. She had spent all her energy and could barely summon the strength to remove her dirty clothes and take a refreshing shower. One hour later, she finally emerged from the changing room clutching her gym bag, her football and her phone.

Practice

Q1. Read the description of how Beth felt again. Underline:
- **(a)** one simile
- **(b)** two adverbs that describe how much
- **(c)** one adverb that describes when
- **(d)** one list
- **(e)** one conjunction.

Q2. Write a short passage of description based on each picture below. Try to include as many different descriptive techniques as you can. Show off your skills!

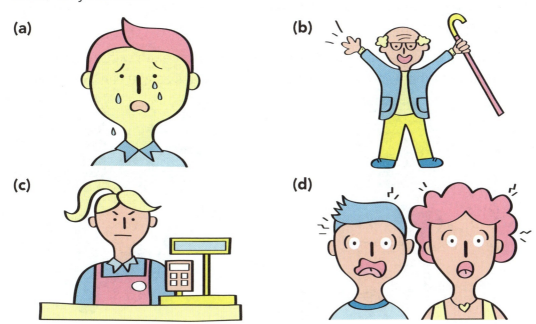

Characters

Your writing task will most likely contain a main character and some side characters too. Writing detailed descriptions of your characters is a great way to make your writing come alive! Read this short passage describing a pirate:

> The pirate's name was Deadly Dave. He was feared across the oceans due to his ruthless character. A bright green parrot perched on his left shoulder and his right eye was made of golden glass. His teeth were as sharp as razors and his voice was deep and rough. He wore a long, black jacket with many patches and pockets. He carried three pistols, four knives and two purple bottles of poison at all times. He loved to swagger confidently across the deck of his ship, Dave's Destroyer.

Helpful Tip...
Did you notice how the names *Deadly Dave* and *Dave's Destroyer* both contain alliteration? Using alliteration when creating names for your characters is a great way to make them memorable for the reader.

Practice

Q1. Read the description of the pirate again. Underline:
   (a) two examples of alliteration (not including the names)
   (b) one simile
   (c) one adverb that describes how something is done.

Q2. Start with your own name and use alliteration to create an interesting character name.

Q3. Write a short passage of description based on each picture below. Try to include as many different descriptive techniques as you can. Show off your skills!

(a)

(b)

(c)

(d)

Settings

The events in your piece of writing will take place within one or more settings. For example, if you are writing a story with the title, 'The Haunted House', it's likely that much of your story will take place within the setting of the haunted house itself.

Writing detailed descriptions of your settings is a great way to make your writing come alive in the reader's mind.

Read this description of a haunted house:

> The humungous house stood at the top of a steep and treacherous mountain. At night, the house's windows glowed fiery orange and steam streamed silently out of its many chimneys as though the house was ablaze. Spooky cackles and howls echoed around the house and the shadows of wispy ghosts could be seen circling it. Few dared to approach as demonic wolves and other ghastly creatures were known to attack anyone foolish enough to ascend the path.

Practice

Q1. Read the description of a Haunted House again. Underline:
- **(a)** two examples of alliteration
- **(b)** one conjunction
- **(c)** two adjectives used to describe the same noun.

Q2. Write a short description based on each picture below.
Try to include as many different descriptive techniques as you can.
Show off your skills!

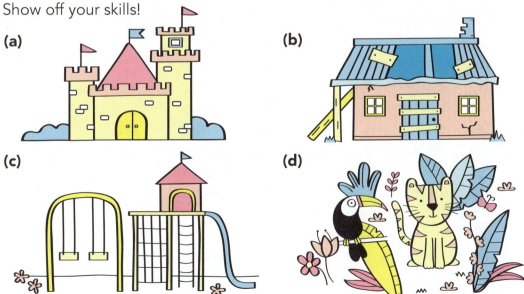

(a) (b) (c) (d)

Spelling

As you saw on page 12, you will be awarded marks for using correct and accurate spelling.

Learning and practising spelling is very important and spelling your words correctly when completing your writing task will make your writing even more impressive!

Helpful Tip...
Whenever you are reading and you come across a new word, jot it down in a notebook. Later on, try to write a sentence or two including the new word. Check your spelling and, if it's incorrect, keep writing sentences until you can confidently spell the new word.

Soon your notebook will be packed full of interesting words and sentences that you can use when completing your writing task.

Practice

Q1. Circle the correctly spelt version of each word.
- **(a)** axident / accident / acident
- **(b)** actual / actul / actuall
- **(c)** disapeer / disapear / disappear
- **(d)** sentense / sentence / sentens
- **(e)** separate / seperate / serparit
- **(f)** concider / consida / consider

Q2. Here are a few words that are often misspelt. For each one, write a sentence including the word and then check whether you have spelt it correctly.

- **(a)** early
- **(b)** island
- **(c)** probably
- **(d)** promise
- **(e)** answer
- **(f)** appear
- **(g)** enough
- **(h)** believe
- **(i)** bicycle
- **(j)** experiment
- **(k)** famous
- **(l)** minute
- **(m)** favourite
- **(n)** naughty
- **(o)** special
- **(p)** caught
- **(q)** centre
- **(r)** strange
- **(s)** opposite
- **(t)** surprise
- **(u)** although
- **(v)** thought
- **(w)** decide
- **(x)** imagine

Q3. Circle the correct spelling in each sentence.

(a) I have **a lot / alot** of homework tonight.
(b) They packed their **possessions / posessions** in cardboard boxes.
(c) I must remember to return my **libarary / library** books.
(d) It took Jasmine a long time to peel all the **potatos / potatoes**.
(e) It is **important / importent** to read a contract before signing it.
(f) "Don't **breath / breathe** a word of this to anyone!" the villain hissed.
(g) Saeed didn't like rock climbing because he was scared of **heights / hights**.
(h) The Roman road was very long and **straight / streight**.
(i) Bill cut the cake into **quarters / quartres**.
(j) I can't **rememeber / remember** what happened that day.

Q4. Read each sentence below.
Put a tick or cross in the box to show whether the underlined word is spelt correctly or not.
Half of them are correct and half are incorrect.

(a) Carla wrote her aunt's address neatly on the envelope. ☐
(b) Vin tried to solve the dificult maths problem. ☐
(c) The gide led them along a narrow, winding path. ☐
(d) It started out as just another ordnary day. ☐
(e) My uncle's knowledge of history is amazing. ☐
(f) The new bookshop was very poplar and always busy. ☐
(g) I would like to paint my room a different colour. ☐
(h) My birthday is in February. ☐
(i) The medcine for my sore throat tasted very bitter. ☐
(j) She wrote the date on her calender. ☐
(k) In the future, I would like to set up my own business. ☐
(l) Fran could feel her heart pounding in her chest. ☐

Handwriting

It's very important that you try to write clearly when completing your writing task. After all, if you write the most amazing, descriptive and imaginative story, it would be a real shame if nobody is able to read it due to poor handwriting!

Look at the following passage:

> The shining sun rose slowly over the mountains and the houses in the valley were soon bathed in light. Sunlight streamed through Katy's window, gently warming her glowing face. Yawning and stretching, she rolled out of bed and strolled over to the bathroom to wash her face. Suddenly, she heard her mum calling from downstairs, "Breakfast is ready!"

Even though the passage is well written, it is difficult to read due to the poor handwriting.

Here is the passage again, this time with good handwriting:

> The shining sun rose slowly over the mountains and the houses in the valley were soon bathed in light. Sunlight streamed through Katy's window, gently warming her glowing face. Yawning and stretching, she rolled out of bed and strolled over to the bathroom to wash her face. Suddenly, she heard her mum calling from downstairs, "Breakfast is ready!"

This is much better! Good handwriting allows the reader to focus on the story rather than struggling to read the words. Remember this next time you complete a piece of writing!

Practice

01. Choose a paragraph from your favourite book and copy it out in your best handwriting.

Checking Your Work

During the writing task, you may finish before the time is up. If you are lucky enough to have some time left over, make sure you use it wisely and check your work! You can often find errors or mistakes that are easily corrected. This will help you to score a higher mark.

Check your work by reading through it carefully. Look out for the issues mentioned in the checklist below:

- Are the words spelt correctly?
- Is there a capital letter at the beginning of every sentence?
- Is there a full stop at the end of every sentence (except where a question mark or exclamation mark is needed)?
- Have speech marks, exclamation marks, question marks and commas been used correctly?
- Have any words been missed by mistake?
- Do the sentences make sense?
- Are the sentences organised into paragraphs?

Practice

Q1. Read through each sentence below. Correct any mistakes that you notice. Use the checklist to help you.

- **(a)** The young man walked down the street happily
- **(b)** Prema and jane visited the museum last week.
- **(c)** The teacher asked the student, "Did you do your homework."
- **(d)** Four men and three women were kaught by the police.
- **(e)** Melvin bought eggs bread and milk from the shop.
- **(f)** Rachel stated that it was the largest mountain that had ever seen.
- **(g)** nobody doubted that Jany would win the competition.
- **(h)** Last year, I eat baked beans for breakfast every day.

Test Practice

Use the following writing tasks to practise all the new skills you have learnt.

Each task should be completed in around 25 minutes.

Task 1

Imagine you are a zookeeper.
You forgot to lock the zoo and all the animals escaped.
Write a story about what you did next.

Task 2

Write a story with the title, 'The Blind Horse'.

Task 3

Tim and Ellen were best friends. Every year, they went on holiday together to the countryside. They loved to take long walks, enjoy the fresh air and pet the animals. It was usually a very relaxing time. However, nothing could have prepared them for the shock they faced on last year's holiday.

Continue the story.

Task 4

Write a story based on the pictures below.

  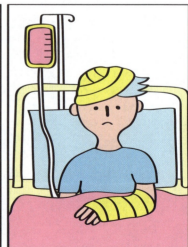

Task 5

Write a diary entry about what you did last weekend.

Task 6

Imagine you are a firefighter. Write a diary entry about a busy day on the job.

Task 7

Imagine you are the first person to land on the planet Mars.
Write a diary entry about your experience.

Task 8

Write a report with the title 'My Favourite Film'.

Task 9

What is your favourite meal?
Write a report about it.

Task 10

Write a report with the title 'My Favourite Toy'.

Answers

Page 13 Understanding the Task

- **Q1.** 30 minutes
- **Q2.** report
- **Q3.** my favourite television show
- **Q4.** I must include a description of the show; and give reasons why I like it.

Pages 14–15 Planning

- **Q1–3** Plans should include details of characters, settings, what happens, the characters' feelings and how the story ends, divided into three clear sections: beginning, middle and end.

Page 16 Paragraphs

- **Q1.** Lines drawn to show two paragraph breaks (three paragraphs), e.g.
Jimy woke up very early in the morning. He excitedly put on his clothes, ate his breakfast and said goodbye to his mother before leaving the house to catch the bus. | When he arrived at the stadium, Jimy found his friends standing outside. They were all as excited as Jimy about the big match. They entered the stadium and took their seats. The match was full of twists and turns and the boys found it very entertaining. Afterwards, Jimy said goodbye to his friends and returned home. | That evening, he helped his mother prepare dinner and they watched a show on the television. Jimy was so exhausted that he fell asleep on the sofa!

Page 17 Past and Present Tense

- **Q1.** past tense
- **Q2.** past tense or present tense
- **Q3.** present tense

Pages 18–19 First and Third Person

- **Q1.** third person
- **Q2.** first person
- **Q3.** first person

Page 20 Conjunctions

- **Q1.** Tim wanted to play football and / but Sara wanted to play rugby.
- **Q2.** The rocket was not built correctly so it crashed into the sea.
- **Q3.** Malik went to the bathroom because / as he wanted to wash his face.
- **Q4.** Ada entered the kitchen and she opened the fridge.
- **Q5.** The dog barked loudly because it saw someone outside.

Page 21 Pronouns

- **Q1.** Gini went to the hospital because she was not feeling well.
- **Q2.** Sam and Tom wolfed down the food because they were hungry.
- **Q3.** The man helped his daughter because she was stuck.
- **Q4.** The builder removed the post so that it was no longer blocking the path.
- **Q5.** I opened the box of chocolates and ate all of them.

Page 22 Sentence Openers

- **Q1.** Suitable sentence openers added to passage, e.g.
Suddenly, Layla heard a knock on the door. Alarmed, she jumped back as she was not expecting anyone. Quietly, she approached the door. Cautiously, she peered through the glass to see who it was. She gasped when she saw the face.

Page 23 Capital Letters and Full Stops

- **Q1.** He wanted to come yesterday but he forgot.
- **Q2.** Helen and Peter struggled to finish the gigantic chocolate cake.
- **Q3.** My best friend went to Paris last year.
- **Q4.** She did not want to go to the cinema but we did.
- **Q5.** Ali decided to stay at home. Oliver decided to go out to play.

7+ CREATIVE WRITING

Page 24 Commas

Q1. The boy put on his gloves, hat and scarf because it was cold outside.

Q2. May wanted to go to the park, the museum and the shops.

Q3. The hungry monkey ate the bananas, the oranges, the apples and the pineapples.

Q4. Raji changed her clothes, brushed her teeth and ate her breakfast.

Q5. The vicious wolf had large claws, thick fur and wicked eyes.

Page 25 Speech Marks

Q1. The astronaut said, "I saw many amazing things in space."

Q2. "Can we listen to the radio?" asked Vin.

Q3. "I simply can't believe it!" Soni exclaimed breathlessly.

Q4. "You may leave once you have cleaned your plate," she declared firmly.

Q5. Rebecca shouted, "I'm coming too!"

Page 26–27 Adjectives

Q1. Suitable adjectives added to passage, e.g.
The dinosaur had razor-sharp claws and teeth. It had large, strong muscles and a long, thick tail. The dinosaur was a ruthless hunter. It used its keen eyes and sensitive nose to hunt for unsuspecting prey. The animals in the jungle all feared the terrible dinosaur and tried to avoid it. Some were luckier than others!

Q2. **good:** amazing, marvellous, fantastic, stupendous, terrific, outstanding
bad: wretched, dreadful, unpleasant, terrible, awful, disagreeable
big: immense, enormous, massive, gigantic, colossal, huge
small: tiny, miniscule, miniature, minute, microscopic, diminutive

Q3. Three alternatives given for each adjective (must have similar meaning), e.g.
(a) **scared:** terrified, frightened, nervous
(b) **happy:** delightful, joyful, cheerful
(c) **sad:** miserable, gloomy, upsetting
(d) **pretty:** beautiful, attractive, appealing
(e) **angry:** annoyed, raging, furious

Page 28–29 Verbs

Q1. Sophie and her friend went on holiday. They spent their days on the beach. They ate ice cream for lunch every day and read lots of interesting books. It was a fantastic holiday!

Q2. Two versions of each sentence containing suitable replacement verbs, e.g.
(a) Fred hopped / hurdled over the wall.
(b) The boy scoffed / nibbled a pancake.
(c) Linda perched / slumped on the chair.
(d) Tariq heaved / tossed the rock into the pond.
(e) Rose was chatting / gossiping with Faisal.

Q3. **walk:** stroll, saunter, strut, shuffle, amble, trudge
run: sprint, bolt, race, dash, scurry, dart
laugh: giggle, chortle, cackle, hoot, chuckle, snicker
cry: weep, wail, sob, bawl, snivel, blubber

Q4. Three alternatives given for each verb (must have similar meaning), e.g.
(a) **look:** peer, gaze, stare
(b) **said:** muttered, whispered, cried
(c) **think:** ponder, muse, consider
(d) **go:** leave, depart, exit

Page 30–31 Adverbs

Q1. Robert swiftly put on his jacket and rushed outside. He could see the light flickering continuously in the distance. He sprinted towards it as quickly as possible.

Q2. Two versions of each sentence containing suitable adverbs, e.g.
(a) The two cats drank the milk thirstily / happily.
(b) Edward strongly / foolishly believed in ghosts.
(c) The young man whistled tunelessly / merrily as he walked across the road.
(d) The bird flew gracefully / desperately from one forest to another.
(e) Sunlight poured brightly / beautifully through the windows into the room.

Q3. **(a)–(l)** Complete sentences that make sense using the given words, e.g. I accidentally knocked over the glass of water.

Page 32–33 Similes

Q1. **(a)–(r)** Complete similes that make sense using the given phrases, e.g. as big as a planet.

Q2. A suitable simile for each picture, e.g.
- **(a)** An ant as big as an elephant.
- **(b)** A boy swimming as fast as a shark.
- **(c)** It is as cold as a snowball.
- **(d)** She is as happy as a young lamb.
- **(e)** A house as small as a box.
- **(f)** A book as colourful as a rainbow.

Q3. **(a)–(r)** Complete sentences that make sense using the given similes, e.g. He sang like an angel.

Page 34–35 Alliteration

Q1. **(a)–(o)** Two adjectives with the same starting sound as the given word, e.g. lazy, lounging lion and slow, slippery snail.

Q2. **(a)–(q)** Complete sentences that make sense using the given phrases, e.g. The caretaker never went anywhere without her trusty tools.

Page 36 Weather

Q1. **(a)** Any two from the following underlined: 'streaked silently', 'wide windscreen', 'great groups of grey clouds gathered'
- **(b)** 'like a growling tiger' underlined
- **(c)** 'suddenly' underlined
- **(d)** 'and' in 'and this was followed' underlined

Q2. **(a)–(d)** A description for each picture containing correct spelling and examples of alliteration, similes, conjunctions and interesting adjectives, verbs and adverbs.

Page 37 Emotions and Feelings

Q1. **(a)** 'like a drum was beating in her head' underlined
- **(b)** Any two from the following underlined: 'completely', 'all', 'barely' Any one from the following
- **(c)** underlined: 'later', 'finally' 'her gym bag, her football and her
- **(d)** phone' underlined 'and' in 'and it felt like' or 'and could
- **(e)** barely' underlined

Q2. **(a)–(d)** A description for each picture containing correct spelling and examples of alliteration, similes, conjunctions and interesting adjectives, verbs and adverbs.

Page 38 Characters

Q1. **(a)** Any two from the following underlined: 'parrot perched', 'golden glass', 'patches and pockets'
- **(b)** 'as sharp as razors' underlined
- **(c)** 'confidently' underlined

Q2. A character name using child's own name and alliteration.

Q3. **(a)–(d)** A description for each picture containing correct spelling and examples of alliteration, similes, conjunctions and interesting adjectives, verbs and adverbs.

Page 39 Settings

Q1. **(a)** 'humungous house' and 'steam streamed silently' underlined
- **(b)** 'and' in 'orange and steam' or 'house and the shadows' or 'as' in 'as demonic wolves' underlined
- **(c)** 'steep' and 'treacherous' underlined

Q2. **(a)–(d)** A description for each picture containing correct spelling and examples of alliteration, similes, conjunctions and interesting adjectives, verbs and adverbs.

Page 40–41 Spelling

Q1.
- **(a)** accident
- **(b)** actual
- **(c)** disappear
- **(d)** sentence
- **(e)** separate
- **(f)** consider

Q2. **(a)–(x)** A sentence written for each given word. The given word must be spelt correctly.

7+ CREATIVE WRITING

Q3.
(a) a lot
(b) possessions
(c) library
(d) potatoes
(e) important
(f) breathe
(g) heights
(h) straight
(i) quarters
(j) remember

Q4.
(a) ✓
(b) ✗
(c) ✗
(d) ✗
(e) ✓
(f) ✗
(g) ✓
(h) ✓
(i) ✗
(j) ✗
(k) ✓
(l) ✓

Page 42 Handwriting

Q1. Child's own choice of passage copied out neatly. It is important that you can clearly read each word.

Page 43 Checking Your Work

Q1.
(a) The young man walked down the street happily.
(b) Prema and Jane visited the museum last week.
(c) The teacher asked the student, "Did you do your homework?"
(d) Four men and three women were caught by the police.
(e) Melvin bought eggs, bread and milk from the shop.
(f) Rebecca stated that it was the largest mountain that she had ever seen.
(g) Nobody doubted that Jany would win the competition.
(h) Last year, I ate baked beans for breakfast every day.

Page 44–45 Test Practice

Use the following checklist to assess your child's response to Tasks 1–10.
Additional guidance is given for each task.

- The instructions provided have been followed / the piece of writing is relevant.
- The piece of writing was completed within the given time.
- The piece of writing has a beginning, middle and end.
- Paragraphs have been used correctly to give the piece of writing structure.
- Correct punctuation has been used, including capital letters, full stops, commas, apostrophes, speech marks and exclamation marks.
- Interesting and exciting adjectives and adverbs have been used.
- Examples of similes and alliteration have been included where appropriate.
- Words are spelt correctly throughout.
- Neat and clear handwriting has been used throughout.

Task 1

- Should be written in first person (consistently).
- Can be written in the past tense (consistently).
- Should begin by explaining the scenario – they are a zookeeper who forgot to lock the zoo and all the animals escaped.
- Should tell the story of what happened next.
- Will ideally include details of how they feel at each stage.

Task 2

- Can be written in past or present tense (consistently).
- Can be written in first or third person (consistently).

Task 3

- Should be written in third person (consistently).
- Can be written in past tense (consistently).
- Should continue directly on from given opening lines.
- Must explain what the shock was (should be something that disrupts Tim and Ellen's usually relaxing holiday).

Task 4

- Must tell the story of a boy being involved in a bike accident and ending up in hospital.

Task 5

- Should be written in first person (consistently).
- Should be written in past tense (consistently).
- Should detail what your child did last weekend.
- Should include personal feelings and opinions.

Task 6

- Should be written in first person (consistently).
- Should be written in past tense (consistently).
- Should take the viewpoint of a firefighter.
- Should detail what happened to the firefighter and how he / she felt about it.

Task 7

- Should be written in first person (consistently).
- Should be written in past tense (consistently).
- Should take the viewpoint of the first person to land on Mars.
- Should describe what happened and include details of feelings and emotions.

Task 8

- Should be written in first person (consistently).
- Should be written in the present tense.
- Should include the name of the film and a description of what it is about.
- Should include reasons why it is their favourite film.

Task 9

- Should be written in first person (consistently).
- Should be written in the present tense.
- Should include a description of the meal.
- Should include reasons why it is / was their favourite meal.

Task 10

- Should be written in first person (consistently).
- Should be written in present tense (consistently).
- Should include a description of their favourite toy.
- Should include reasons why it is their favourite toy.

Glossary

Adjective – Adjectives describe or give extra information about a person or thing (noun), e.g. He had **long**, **brown** hair.

Adverb – Adverbs give information about an action (verb), e.g. She jogged **slowly** across the field.

Alliteration – Alliteration is the use of several words close together that all begin with the same sound, e.g. The silent, slithering serpent made its way slowly to the sea.

Capital letter – A capital letter is used at the beginning of a new sentence and at the beginning of names of people and places, e.g. The train carried Jan through the countryside towards London.

Character – The characters in a story are the people who it is about.

Comma – Commas are used to separate the items in a list, except for the last two items, which are separated by the word 'and', e.g. I bought three pencils, two pens, an eraser and a ruler.

Comprehension – Comprehension is the ability to understand something. Comprehension tasks in exams usually include a piece of text followed by questions that test how well you have understood the text.

Conclusion – The conclusion of a piece of writing is the ending. In a story, it tells the reader what happened to the characters. In a report, it might remind the reader of the key points.

Conjunction – A conjunction is a word that joins together sentences, e.g. The boy was crying **because** he had lost his dog.

Description – A description is a 'picture' created using words, e.g. The stranger was tall and very thin. He walked with a slight stoop, like a willow shoot bending in the breeze.

Diary entry – A diary entry is a personal record of the things that happened during the course of a day.

Emotion – An emotion is a feeling, such as happiness, love, fear or anger.

Feelings – Your feelings about something are the things that you think and feel about it.

Fiction – Fiction refers to stories that are about imaginary characters and events (rather than real people and events).

First person – When you write in the first person, you are writing about yourself and your thoughts and feelings, using words such as *I, me, my, mine, we, us* and *ours*. A story can be written in the first person if you put yourself in the position of the main character and describe what is happening from their viewpoint.

Full stop – A full stop is used at the end of a sentence, e.g. Mandeep didn't want the evening to end.

Logical – Something that is logical is sensible. Writing is organised in a logical way if one idea leads on to another in a way that makes sense to the reader.

Non-fiction – Non-fiction refers to writing that is about real characters and events (rather than imaginary people and events). The details in non-fiction are facts.

Noun – A noun is a word that refers to a person or thing, e.g. 'car', 'John' and 'love'.

Noun phrase – A noun phrase is a noun plus the words that describe it, e.g. 'an apple', 'my brother', 'the big, black spider'.

Opinions – Your opinion about something is what you think or believe about it.

Paragraph – A paragraph is a section of writing. Paragraphs are used to give a piece of writing structure. A paragraph always begins on a new line.

Past tense – You use past tense to write about things that happened in the past, e.g. This morning, I missed my bus so I was late for school.

Present tense – You use the present tense to write about things that are happening now, including thoughts and feelings, e.g. I don't like chocolate flavoured ice cream.

Pronoun – A pronoun is a word that you use to refer to someone or something without using a noun. Pronouns include *I, me, she, he, we, they, it, hers, his, theirs, them* and *they*.

Punctuation – Punctuation refers to the symbols that we use to write sentences correctly and clearly, e.g. full stops, commas, speech marks, question marks and exclamation marks.

Question mark – A question mark (?) is used at the end of a sentence to show that it is a question.

Report – A report is a formal piece of writing that gives information about a subject you are interested in.

Sentence – A sentence is a group of words that begins with a capital letter and ends with a full stop, question mark or exclamation mark. A sentence contains a subject and a verb.

Sentence opener – A sentence opener is a word or phrase used at the beginning of a sentence to help show the order of things or link two ideas, e.g. **First**, I wrote a plan. **Then**, I began to write my story.

Setting – The setting is the place where the events of a story take place.

Simile – A simile is a descriptive technique. It compares one thing to another using the word 'like' or 'as', e.g. as cool as a cucumber.

Speech marks – Speech marks are used to show which words in a piece of writing are spoken by a character, e.g. "I would love to come to your party!" squealed Katy.

Story – A story is a description of imaginary people and events. It has a beginning, middle and end.

Suspense – Suspense is when a piece of writing makes the reader interested and excited to know what happens next.

Third person – When you write in the third person, you are writing about another person, using words such as *she, he* and *they*. A story is written in the third person if you write as if you are observing the characters and events.

Verb – A verb is a word that names an action, e.g. Suni **ran** as fast as she could.

Viewpoint – Viewpoint refers to the position you take when writing. For example, you might write from your own viewpoint (describing your thoughts, feelings and experiences) or you might put yourself in the position of a character and write as if you were them (describing their thoughts, feelings and experiences).

Vocabulary – Vocabulary refers to the words that you know and use. In the writing exam, it is important to use a wide vocabulary, i.e. a range of interesting words.

Notes

Notes

Notes

ACKNOWLEDGEMENTS

Developed by Letts Educational in partnership with Exam Papers Plus (www.exampapersplus.co.uk) to benefit from their combined curriculum knowledge and assessment expertise.

The authors and publisher are grateful to the copyright holders for permission to use quoted materials and images.

Every effort has been made to trace copyright holders and obtain their permission for the use of copyright material. The author and publisher will gladly receive information enabling them to rectify any error or omission in subsequent editions. All facts are correct at time of going to press.

Published by Letts Educational
An imprint of HarperCollins*Publishers*
1 London Bridge Street
London SE1 9GF

ISBN: 978-1-84419-903-7

First published 2018

10 9 8 7 6 5 4 3

© HarperCollins*Publishers* Limited 2018

All rights reserved. No part of this publication may be reproduced, stored in a retrieval system, or transmitted, in any form or by any means, electronic, mechanical, photocopying, recording or otherwise, without the prior permission of Letts Educational.

British Library Cataloguing in Publication Data.

A CIP record of this book is available from the British Library.

Commissioning Editors: Michelle I'Anson and Alison James
Author: Faisal Nasim, Exam Papers Plus
Editor and Project Manager: Rebecca Skinner
Reviewer: Graham Spooner, The Sensible Tuition Company
Cover Design: Sarah Duxbury
Inside Concept Design, Text Design and Layout: Fixate
Production: Natalia Rebow
Printed in Great Britain by Martins the Printers

MIX
Paper from responsible source
www.fsc.org FSC C007454

This book is produced from independently certified FSC™ paper to ensure responsible forest management.

For more information visit:
www.harpercollins.co.uk/green